CONTENTS

OBJECTIVES 2
RULES 2
PONY CLUB POLOCROSS.. 3
PART 1 – GENERAL ....CROSSE. 4
1. SYNOPSIS OF 4
2. DRESS 6
3. SADDLERY 10
4. INSPECTION 14
5. ACTION AFTER 14
6. HEAD INJURIES .... SION 14
7. MEDICAL SUSPEN 17
8. UNSEEMLY BEHAVIOUR 17
9. PERFORMANCE-ENHANCING DRUGS 18
10. DISQUALIFICATION 19
11. SPONSORSHIP 19
12. INSURANCE 20
13. HEALTH AND SAFETY 20
14. LEGAL LIABILITY 20
15. SPECTATOR AREAS 20

PART 2 – RULES FOR THE PONY CLUB POLOCROSSE CHAMPIONSHIPS 21
16. ELIGIBILITY 21
17. MIXED/AREA TEAMS/SECTIONS 22
18. BRANCH/CENTRE/AREA MANAGERS 22
19. CHAMPIONSHIP CLASSES 22
20. ENTRIES 23
21. WITHDRAWALS (for all Competitions) 24
22. ABANDONMENT (for all Competitions) 24
23. MEASUREMENT OF PONIES/HORSES 24
24. OBJECTIONS AND PROTESTS 24
25. TACK AND TURNOUT 25

PART 3 – PLAYING RULES 25
26. INSTRUCTIONS FOR GOAL JUDGES 30
27. POLOCROSSE FIELD 31
28. EXAMPLE OF FIELD RULES 32

APPENDICES 34
APPENDIX A – HEAD INJURY AND CONCUSSION FLOWCHART 34
APPENDIX B – SUGGESTED KEY FOR LEAGUE TOURNAMENTS 35

OBJECTIVES

Polocrosse provides The Pony Club with a team competition requiring courage, determination and all-round riding ability on the part of the rider, and careful and systematic training of the pony. It encourages a higher standard of riding throughout The Pony Club and to stimulate among the future generation a greater interest in riding as a sport and as a recreation. I is suitable for ordinary children on ordinary ponies and encourages a strong and unselfish team spirit.

"As a Member of The Pony Club, I stand for the best in sportsmanship as we as in horsemanship.

I shall compete for the enjoyment of the game well played and take winning or losing in my stride, remembering that without good manners and good temper, sport loses its cause for being. I shall at all times treat my horse with due consideration."

RULES

Except where varied below, these competitions are conducted under the UK Polocrosse Association and International Polocrosse Council Rules, copies of these rules can be found at ukpolocrosse.co.uk

Every eventuality cannot be provided for in these rules. In any unforeseen or exceptional circumstances or any other issue in connection with Pony Club Polocrosse, it is the duty of the relevant officials to make a decision in a sporting spirit and to approach as nearly as possible the intention of these rules. It is the competitors' responsibility to ensure that they are complying with the rules of the competition.

Please see the Polocrosse pages of pcuk.org for details of training days and tournaments guidelines for tournament organisers and hints for young players

NOTE: Rules which differ from those of 2022 appear in bold type and sidelined (as this note).

Rulebook Version: 23.1.0

PONY CLUB POLOCROSSE COMMITTEE

Chairman

- Iain Heaton
  pxchairman@pcuk.org

Members

- Laura Scott
- Natalie Harpin
- Pam Drew
- Angela Fynn
- Jo Gale
- Lucinda Hayes
- Hetta Wilkinson (Area Representative)

Sports Development Officer: polocrosse@pcuk.org

Health & Safety: safety@pcuk.org

The Pony Club
Lowlands Equestrian Centre, Old Warwick Road, Warwick, CV35 7AX
Tel: 02476 698300
pcuk.org

Please see the Polocrosse pages of pcuk.org for:

- Details of training days and tournaments

All Rules are made by The Pony Club Polocrosse Committee, with consultation of other volunteer committees where relevant.

The Pony Club Office provides administrative support and any queries or questions relating to these rules must be directed to the Chairman of the relevant sport,

© 2023 The Pony Club

All rights reserved. No part of this publication may be reproduced, stored in a retrieval system, or transmitted, in any form or by means, electronic, mechanical, photocopying, recording or otherwise without the prior permission of The Pony Club.

PART 1 – GENERAL RULES FOR PONY CLUB POLOCROSSE

1. SYNOPSIS OF THE GAME

As the name implies Polocrosse is a combination of polo and lacrosse. It is a team game on horseback and the aim is to score goals. The team that scores the most goals in a match is the winner.

a) **Equipment** – each player has a stick made up of a shaft which is attached to a head with a loose twisted-thread net in which the ball is carried. The stick is usually 1m to 1.2m (39" to 42") long, but there is no restriction in length. The ball is made of foam rubber, approximately 10cm (4") in diameter, and weighs approximately 142g (5 oz).

b) **The Field** – should be reasonably flat. It is 146.5m (160yds) long by 55m (60yds) wide, with goal posts 2.5m (8ft) apart at each end.

27.5m (30yds) from each end there is a line across the field which is called the penalty or 30 yard line and enclosed the goal scoring area. Directly in front of each goal there is a semi-circle of 10m (11yds) radius. A goal can only be scored if it is thrown from outside this semi-circle, but inside the goal scoring area.

c) **Teams and sections** – a section consists of three players and a full Branch/Centre team consists of six players. In a full team the two sections play alternate chukkas so that any time while the match is in progress three players are on the field of play and the other three are resting. There can be 4, 6 or 8 chukkas in a match.

Tournaments can also be played with sections of just three players, in which case it is usual to have three chukka matches. Also sometimes at a one day tournament there will be one or two chukka matches.

The members of each section are numbered 1, 2 and 3 and must wear shirts or tabards with these numbers clearly on them.

- No. 1 is attack, and is the only player that can score a goal for their section, and the only one that can play in their goal scoring area. They can play in the centre field, but may not play in the goal scoring area their team is defending.
- No. 2 may only play in the centre area between the two penalty lines.
- No. 3 is defence and plays in the centre area and the goal scoring area that they are defending.

Thus only the attacking No. 1 and defending No. 3 are allowed in the respective goal scoring areas.

d) **Ponies** – a player is allowed only one pony in a class, unless this rule is specifically altered for a tournament by the Pony Club Polocrosse Committee to allow multiple horses to be used.

e) **The Start** – the game is commenced in centre field, the players lining up in pairs side by side and one behind the other, each team standing closest to the goal it is defending. The No. 1's are in front, then the No. 2's and the No. 3's are at the back, all facing the umpire and at least 3m from him. The umpire throws the ball in overarm from the side line straight between the players. The ball should be thrown at a height between the players' shoulders and the maximum possible height of their sticks. This is so that it is catchable by all the players. The game recommences similarly after a goal is scored from alternate sides of the field.

Whenever an attempt at goal fails, No. 3 throws the ball back into play from just behind the 30 yd penalty line.

f) **Play** – players pick up the ball from the ground, or catch it in the net of the stick and carry it or throw it from player to player until the No. 1 (attack) is in possession of it in the goal scoring area, so as to be able to throw at goal. A player cannot carry the ball over the penalty line, but must bounce it on the ground, so that he does not have possession of it while crossing the line. However, he may throw the ball to another player across the line.

A player carrying the ball in his stick must carry it on his stick side, i.e. right-handed players carry it on the off side of the pony, left-handed players on the near-side. A player cannot carry it across his pony, but he can pick up or catch the ball on the non-stick side provided he brings the stick back to his stick side immediately.

Hitting at an opponent's stick, either to dislodge the ball or prevent him from gaining possession of it, is allowed in an upward direction only Hitting down is not allowed as the pony might be hit.

"Riding-off" is allowed, but crossing, stopping over the ball, or elbowing are not allowed. The wedging or sandwiching of one player between two players "riding-off" simultaneously is dangerous play and not allowed.

g) **Time** – the maximum length of a chukka is 8 minutes but usually 6 minutes is normal, and there is a 2 minute change over time between chukkas. Each section of a team will play in the opposite direction in successive chukkas.

Matches can be of 2, 4, 6 or a maximum of 8 chukkas.

2. DRESS

New equipment is not expected, but what is worn must be clean, neat, tidy and safe.

It is the competitor's responsibility to ensure their dress complies with the Rules. Contravention may incur disqualification.

a) Hats and Hair

Hair: Must be tied back securely, in a safe manner to reduce the risk of hair being caught and to prevent scalp injuries.

It is mandatory for all Members to wear a protective helmet at all times when mounted with the chinstrap fastened and adjusted so as to prevent movement of the hat in the event of a fall. This rule defines the quality of manufacture that is required. Individual Sports may also have additional requirements with regard to colour and type of hat. It is strongly recommended that second-hand hats are not purchased.

The hat standards accepted are detailed in the table below:

Hat Standard	Safety Mark	Allowed at the following activities:
PAS 015 2011 with BSI Kitemark		All activities
VG1 with BSI Kitemark		All activities
Snell E2016 onwards with the official Snell label and number		All activities
ASTM-F1163 2004a onwards with the SEI mark		All activities
AS/NZS 3838, 2006 onwards		All activities

- For cross country riding (80cm and over) including Eventing, Tetrathlon, Horse Trials, Pony Racing (whether it be tests, rallies, competition or training) and Mounted Games competitions, a jockey skull cap must be worn with no fixed peak, peak type extensions or noticeable protuberances above the eyes or to the front, and should have an even round or elliptical shape with a smooth or slightly abrasive surface.

Noticeable protuberances above the eyes or to the front not greater than 5mm, smooth and rounded in nature are permitted. A removable hat cover with a light flexible peak may be used if required.

- It is strongly recommended that a jockey skull cap is worn for cross country riding over lower fences (less than 80cm).
- No recording device is permitted (e.g. hat cameras) as they may have a negative effect on the performance of the hat in the event of a fall.
- The fit of the hat and the adjustment of the harness are as crucial as the quality. Members are advised to try several makes to find the best fit. The hat should not move on the head when the head is tipped forward. Most helmet manufacturers recommend you visit a qualified BETA fitter.
- Hats must be replaced after a severe impact as subsequent protection will be significantly reduced. Hats deteriorate with age and should be replaced after three to five years depending upon the amount of use.
- Hats must be worn at all times (including at prize-giving) when mounted with the chinstrap fastened and adjusted so as to prevent movement of the hat in the event of a fall.
- The Official Steward/Organiser may, at his discretion, eliminate a competitor riding in the area of the competition without a hat or with the chinstrap unfastened or with a hat that does not comply with these standards.

Hat Checks and Tagging

The Pony Club and its Branches and Centres will appoint Officials, who are familiar with The Pony Club hat rule, to carry out hat checks and tag each hat that complies with the requirements set out in the hat rule with a **pink** Pony Club hat tag. Hats fitted with a **pink** Pony Club, British Eventing (BE) or British Riding Club (BRC) hat tag will not need to be checked on subsequent occasions. However, The Pony Club reserves the right to randomly spot check any hat regardless of whether it is already tagged.

Pony Club (**Pink**) hat tags are only available to purchase from The Pony Club Shop.

Tagging indicates that a hat meets the accepted standards. No check of the fit and condition of the hat is implied. It is considered to be the responsibility of the Member's parent(s)/guardian(s) to ensure that their child's hat complies with the required standards and is tagged before they go to any Pony Club event. They are also responsible for ensuring that the manufacturer's guidelines with regard to fit and replacement are followed.

b) **Face Guards** – are recommended. If they are worn they must be fitted to a Pony Club approved hat.

c) **Jewellery** – the wearing of any sort of jewellery when handling or riding a horse/pony is not recommended and if done at any Pony Club activity, is done at the risk of the member/their parent/guardian. However, to stop any risk of injury, necklaces and bracelets (other than medical bracelets) must be removed, as must larger and more pendulous pieces of jewellery (including those attached to piercings) which create a risk of injury to the body part through which they are secured. For the avoidance of doubt a wristwatch, wedding ring, stock pin worn horizontally and/or a tie clip are permitted. It is recommended that stock pins are removed for cross country.

d) **Breeches** – white, cream or beige jodhpurs, white riding trousers or white jeans must be worn. (Long boots, 1/2 chaps to be worn with trousers/breeches).

e) **Spurs** – may be worn at Rallies and other events. Any misuse of spurs will be reported to the DC/Centre Proprietor, Area Representative and Training Chairman; any reported riders will be recorded and monitored.

Sharp spurs are not permitted. Only blunt spurs, without rowels or sharp edges, and spurs that have a smooth rotating ball on the shank may be worn. If the spurs are curved, the curve must be downwards and the shank must point straight to the back and not exceed 4cm in length. The measurement is taken from the boot to the end of the shank.

Spurs must only be used to enhance the normal leg aids and allow for better communication from rider to horse.

Spurs must never be used to vent a competitor's anger or to reprimand the horse.

Use of the spurs which causes injury eg. blood, broken skin or a weal, is always classed as misuse.

Misuse of the spurs anywhere at the event will result in disqualification.

f) **Footwear** – Only standard riding or jodhpur boots with a well-defined square cut heel may be worn. Plain black or brown half chaps may be worn with jodhpur boots of the same colour. Tassels and fringes are not allowed. No other footwear will be permitted, including wellington boots, yard boots, country boots, "muckers" or trainers. Boots with interlocking treads are not permitted, nor are the boots or treads individually.

Stirrups should be of the correct size to suit the rider's boots (see the Stirrup rule). Laces on boots must be taped for Mounted Games only.

g) **Knee pads** – if used must be made of soft fabric or leather and must be pliable.

h) No player may wear buckles or studs on the upper part of his boots or knee pads in such a way as could damage another player, their boots or breeches or their horse.

i) **Numbers** – shirts or tabards numbered 1, 2 and 3 must be worn to indicate the position of the player. The number should be clearly visible on the back of the shirt, and on the sleeve if desired. The only other writing permitted is the name of the Branch/Centre and the logo on the front pocket. Teams should be in matching colours and wear matching tabards.

j) **Body Protector Rule**

The Pony Club follows British Equestrian standards for Body Protectors.

The use of body protectors is compulsory for all Cross Country riding and Pony Racing in both training or competing. If a Body protector is worn for any Pony Club activity it must meet BETA 2009 Level 3 standard (purple label) or BETA 2018 Level 3 standard (blue and black label) – see right.

For general use, the responsibility for choosing body protectors and the decision as to their use must rest with Members and their parents. It is recommended that a rider's body protector should not be more than 2% of their body weight. When worn, body protectors must fit correctly, be comfortable and must not restrict movement. BETA recommends body protectors are replaced at least every three to five years, after which the impact absorption properties of the foam may have started to decline.

BETA 2009 Level 3 (purple label) body protectors will continue to be accepted at Pony Club competitions until 31st December 2023, from 1st January 2024 only body protectors that meet BETA 2018 Level 3 standard (blue and black label) are to be used.

Riders who choose to use the Woof Wear Body Cage EXO must lodge a key with the Event Organiser when they collect their number.

Air Jackets

The Pony Club follows the British Equestrian Standards for Air Jackets.

If a rider chooses to wear an air jacket, it must only be used in addition to a normal body protector which meets the Body Protector Rule and Standards. In the event of a fall, the air jacket must be fully deflated or removed before continuing, after which, the conventional body protector will continue to give protection. Air jackets must not be worn under a jacket and number bibs should be fitted loosely or with elasticated fastenings over the air jacket. Sports have specific rules relating to falls in competition.

3. SADDLERY

Ponies must be turned out with well-fitting and properly maintained black brown tack. New equipment is not expected, but what is worn must be clean, neat, tidy and safe.

It is the competitor's responsibility to ensure their tack complies with the Rules. Contravention may incur disqualification.

The Chief Umpire has absolute discretion to forbid the use of any bit, gadget, spur or boot which he considers cruel or misused. Any misuse of the bit/ bridle will be reported to the District Commissioner/Centre Proprietor, Area Representative and Training Chairman. Any reported riders will be recorded and monitored.

Any equipment not covered in these rules must be referred at least two weeks in advance of the competition to The Pony Club Office to allow time for the Chairman of the Polocrosse Committee to be consulted.

Breast plates to be worn at all levels and should be fitted to a plain black/ brown saddle. Buckled saddlery is strongly recommended. Any clips on tack must be taped for safety reasons. Tack officials have the final say.

a) **Saddles** – stock saddles are by no means required, but may be used (without a roping horn) in the Junior and Senior classes. Open ended stirrup bars are recommended, with any safety clips in the down position, but if stirrup leathers are attached permanently to the tree then caged stirrups are recommended. All saddles should fit the horse correctly and all saddles and leathers should be in a safe and sound condition.

Humane Girths

Humane girths pose an increased risk as many common designs may have complete girth failure if a single strap was to break. Humane girths are not permitted in any Sport, whether during training or competition.

b) **Stirrups -** Stirrups should be of the correct size to suit the rider's boots. They must have 7mm (¼") clearance on either side of the boot. To find this measurement, tack checkers should move the foot across to one side of the stirrup, with the widest part of the foot on the tread. From the side of the boot to the edge of the stirrup should not be less than 14mm.

There are now many types of stirrups marketed as 'safety stirrups'. All riders must ensure that their stirrups are suitable for the type of footwear they are wearing and the activities in which they are taking part and that the stirrup leathers are in good condition.

There are no prescribed weight limits on metal stirrups, however with the advent of stirrups of other materials, weight limits are frequently given by manufacturers. Any person buying these stirrups, should comply with weight limits defined on the box or attached information leaflets. Neither the feet nor the stirrup leathers or irons, may be attached to the girth, nor the feet attached to the stirrup irons.

It is strongly recommended that the design of the stirrup chosen allows the foot to be released easily in the event of a rider fall.

Particular focus should be on ensuring that the boot and stirrup are the correct size for the rider taking part and used in line with the manufacturer's guidance.

For the avoidance of doubt, at Pony Club events:

- stirrups which connect the boot and the stirrup magnetically are not allowed
- Interlocking boot soles and stirrup treads are not allowed

Stirrups that equipment could become caught in, such as open sided stirrups, will not be permitted.

Peacock stirrups with rubber band or leather strap (pictured below) are not allowed.

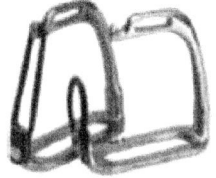

c) **Bridles** – plain black or brown leather bridles only be used.

d) **Blinkers** – are not allowed, nor is any form of noseband or cheeks that obstructs the vision of the pony. Eye protection is allowed provided it doesn't restrict the horse's vision.

e) **Numnahs, Saddle Cloths, Blankets** – any solid colour is permitted. Contrasting piping is permitted. Branch logos are allowed when competing for the Branch; logos must not exceed 200 sq. cm.

This does not preclude the wearing of clothing for horses or riders that has been presented by sponsors of the Championships in the current or previous years.

f) **Market Harboroughs** and running, draw or check reins of any kind are forbidden.

g) The use of string, twine or cord in or around the horse's mouth is forbidden.

h) **Martingales** – standing or running martingales are permitted. Standing martingales may be attached only to a cavesson noseband or the cavesson portion of a flash noseband fitted above the bit.

i) **Nosebands** – only one noseband may be worn unless using a standing martingale with a combination, kineton, drop noseband or similar in which case the addition of a cavesson is allowed. Nosebands must be correctly fitted and should not cause discomfort. Chain nosebands are not permitted. Rope or rawhide nosebands are permitted but leather nosebands are recommended.

j) **Bits** – bits with cheek pieces that protrude below the ring that the rein is attached to are not permitted. In all cases the mouthpiece must be smooth. In the opinion of the Chief Umpire and the Tack Officials, bits deemed to be excessively thin in the mouthpiece will not be accepted.

k) **Reins** – to be of black or brown leather, or white, black or brown cotton. No bridge reins allowed.

l) **Boots and Bandages** – ponies' legs must be correctly bandaged with gamgee type material protecting the fetlock and pastern, or properly fitting polo bandages, or have suitable boots which protect the fetlock.

Over-reach boots, both in front and behind, are compulsory. Hoof boots, without buckles or protrusions, are permitted.

m)   **Studs**
  i. Only one recognised stud without a hard centre of ½ inch (13mm) cubed can be fitted to the outside of each hind shoe within 1 inch (25mm) of the heel. The studs should not be placed at the widest part of the shoe. This is the recommended method.
  ii. Road nails with a hardened tip are allowed on the outside of each hind shoe. Frost nails and screws are not allowed.
  iii. Ponies found with the incorrect studs will not be allowed to play until the studs are removed.

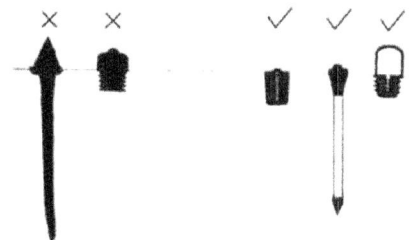

n)   **Whips** – must not be longer than 1.1m (44") including a flap not less than 50mm (2") long and 25mm (1") wide at the end.

At all times, the whip must only be used:

- For a good reason, as an aid to encourage the horse forward.
- At an appropriate time, namely when the horse is reluctant to go forward under normal aids of seat and legs.
- In the right place, namely down the shoulder or behind the leg but never overarm.
- With appropriate severity.
- No more than twice for any one incident.

Excessive use of the whip anywhere at the event will result in disqualification:

- Use of the whip to vent a competitor's anger is always excessive.
- Use of a whip which causes injury eg. Broken skin or a weal, is always excessive.
- Use after elimination or retirement is always excessive.
- Use on a horse's head, neck etc. is always excessive.
- Using the whip from the ground after a rider fall or dismount is always excessive.
- If the rider's arm comes above the shoulder when using the whip, this is always excessive.

o) **Electronic Devices –** (i.e. headphones, mobile phones etc. enabling another person to communicate with the rider) are not allowed whilst the rider is competing. No recording device is permitted (e.g. head/bridle cameras etc.).

p) Competitors using saddlery and gadgets which are not allowed in the competition may be eliminated, except that lungeing in side reins, but NOT bearing, check or balancing reins, is permitted.

q) No item of tack may be used for any other purpose, or in any other way than that for which it was designed and intended, e.g. running martingales may not be used as standing martingales.

r) Badly fitting or unsafe tack, or saddles that are down on the withers when the rider is mounted, will result in the disqualification of that competitor, unless the tack can be changed to the satisfaction of the Chief Umpire before the start of the game. The Chief Umpire has absolute discretion in ruling on these matters.

s) **Prize Giving –** only tack that falls within the rules of the competition should be allowed for prize giving. All teams should be dressed in full riding gear.

4. INSPECTION

Riders and ponies will be inspected in the clothing and saddlery in which they are to ride, and these will not be changed thereafter without reference to the Chief Umpire. Tack Stewards will report any rider whom they think may be overweight for their pony to the Chief Umpire. Team Managers must accompany their team and ensure they are presented at the appointed time for their tack inspection, ready to play.

5. ACTION AFTER A FALL

Any competitor who has a fall or sustains a serious injury anywhere at the competition site MUST see the medical personnel on the day and be passed fit to ride before riding that horse in a further chukka or before riding any other horse.

6. HEAD INJURIES AND CONCUSSION

There are strict procedures around the response to concussion.

(i) General Advice

Head injuries and concussion can be life changing and fatal. Serious head injuries are usually obvious, but concussion can be very subtle. It may not be immediately apparent but should be taken very seriously.

Members may be asked not to ride by an Official (including a first aider) who believes they may have sustained a concussion either at the time of injury or from a previous injury (which may not have been sustained whilst riding). Concussion is difficult to diagnose, and practitioners of all grades must err on the side of caution. Thus, any decision must be respected, and professional medical support is advised to avoid further harm. Ignoring an official's advice about concussion would breach the Pony Club's Code of Conduct.

(ii) Incidents that could cause head injuries or concussion

Any Member who suffers an incident that could cause head injury or concussion at a Pony Club activity (for example, a fall from their horse/pony) should be assessed by the first aid provider in attendance.

Dependent on the level of first aid cover, the exact process of diagnosing will vary depending/based on whether the Member has suffered:

- No head injury/concussion
- Suspected head injury/concussion
- Confirmed head injury/concussion

The process for diagnosing each option is talked through in more detail below.

From the assessment being carried out it may be immediately obvious that there is no cause for concern. Reasonable care should be taken to ensure Members have not sustained a serious head injury or concussion.

(iii) Unconsciousness

If a Member is unconscious following an incident they should be treated as if they are suffering with a confirmed concussion and the steps in point vii should be followed.

(iv) Who can diagnose head injury or concussion?

Diagnosis of a head injury or concussion can be carried out by any level of first aid cover officiating at a Pony Club activity. Trainer or Qualified First Aiders will only be able to diagnose a suspected head injury or concussion. If there is any doubt as to the diagnosis, the Member should see the highest level of first aid cover that is present, and they should make the diagnosis. If unable to reach a definite diagnosis or the first aider is the highest level of cover at the activity, then the Member should be referred to a hospital or a doctor off site for a professional diagnosis.

The member must not ride again until they have been seen by a doctor/hospital.

(v) Actions to be taken in the event of a suspected head injury or suspected concussion diagnosis

If a diagnosis of a suspected head injury or concussion is made by a first aider, the parents/guardians should be advised to take the member to hospital.

Any Member who has been diagnosed with a suspected or confirmed head injury/concussion should not be left alone and must be returned to the care of their parents/guardians where appropriate.

If a Member has a suspected head injury/concussion at an activity/competition, organisers should inform the DC/Proprietor to ensure that the rider follows these guidelines.

Once a diagnosis of suspected head injury or concussion is made by the first aid cover present at the activity, then that decision is final. If a Member is advised to see a doctor because of suspected head injury/concussion and the parents/guardians decide not to allow the member to be examined (either at the activity or in hospital), the Member will not be allowed to ride again on the day and should be treated as if they have sustained a confirmed head injury/concussion. Depending on the circumstances, the decision not to allow further examination may be considered a safeguarding issue.

Where a doctor subsequently certifies that a Member does not have or did not suffer a head injury/concussion, and provides evidence that they are satisfied the Member is well enough to continue, that Member will be treated as if they did not sustain a concussion and may continue. Officials will endeavour to assess members in a timely way; however, head injuries can evolve over time, which may lead an official or professional to perform a series of assessments. A Member may miss a phase or part of an event during the assessment process and the Sport Rules for missing that phase or part will apply.

(vi) Actions to be taken in the event of a confirmed head injury or confirmed concussion

In the event of a confirmed head injury or confirmed concussion diagnosis, the doctor will advise the Member not to ride or take part in any activity that potentially involves hard contact for three weeks. The member may be advised that they could request a review of any ongoing concussion problems by a doctor (with experience in assessing concussion) after 10 days. If that doctor is happy to certify that the Member is not suffering with a concussion, the Member may ride again. Evidence regarding this decision is required, e.g. in the form of a medical letter. If no evidence is provided, the Member should not take part in any Pony Club activity that involves horses/ponies, whether mounted or unmounted, for at least three weeks after the initial injury.

(vii) Actions to be taken in the event of a diagnosis of a confirmed or suspected head injuries/concussions outside of Pony Club activities

Ultimately, it is the parents/guardians responsibility to make a decision about the welfare of their child.

If a Pony Club Official becomes aware that a member has sustained a suspected or confirmed head injury/concussion and has been advised not to take part in any potentially hard contact activities, the Member must not be allowed to take part in any Pony Club activities that involves horses/ponies, whether mounted or unmounted for three weeks, unless appropriate medical evidence of fitness to ride can be provided by parents/guardians dated at least 10 days after the initial injury.

Please see Appendix A for the Head Injury and Concussion Flowchart.

7. MEDICAL SUSPENSION

If a Member has been suspended from taking part in any activity/competition/sport for medical reasons, this suspension must apply **to** all Pony Club activities until such time the Member is passed fit by a medical professional to take part. It is the Member and parent/guardian's responsibility to ensure this rule is adhered to.

Medical letters are required, following a suspension for medical reasons, to allow a Member to take part in any activity again. The letter should be issued by the either the hospital or specialist(s) involved in treating the injury, where appropriate.

8. UNSEEMLY BEHAVIOUR

Unseemly behaviour on the part of riders, team officials, or team supporters will be reported as soon as possible to The Pony Club Office. Offenders may be penalised by disqualification of the Branch or Branches concerned for a period up to three years. Any competitor who in the opinion of the Official Umpire or Organiser, has been extremely rude or aggressive towards any officials at a competition, or who has behaved in an aggressive or unfair manner to their horse, may be disqualified.

9. PERFORMANCE-ENHANCING DRUGS

All performance-enhancing drugs are strictly forbidden and The Pony Club supports 100% clean sport.

(i) Equine – Controlled Medication

It is clearly essential for the welfare of a horse/pony that appropriate veterinary treatment is given if and when required, including appropriate medication. However, medication may mask an underlying health problem. Therefore, horses should not compete or take part in training activities when taking medication, if the combination of the medication and the activity may have a detrimental effect on the horse's welfare. Therapeutic Use Exemptions (TUE) should be confirmed in writing by a Vet.

For more information, please refer to the Welfare of Horses and Ponies at Pony Club Activities Policy, available on The Pony Club website.

(ii) Human

Performance-enhancing drugs are forbidden. The Pony Club supports the approach taken by the UK Anti-Doping Agency in providing clean sport. The Pony Club disciplinary procedures would be used in cases where doping may be suspected including reporting to the UK Anti-Doping Agency.

(iii) Testing

All competitors should be aware that random samples may be taken for testing from both themselves and/or their horse/pony. The protocol used will be that of the relevant adult discipline.

Competitors and their horses/ponies at national or international level may be subject to blood tests in line with the Sports Council Policy on illegal and prescribed substances. All young people competing at these levels should be made aware of this

Reporting

i. Anyone who has reasonable grounds for suspecting that a Member is using or selling an illegal substance must report their concerns to the District Commissioner/Centre Proprietor as soon as practicable. If there is an immediate risk to the health, safety or welfare of one or more Members then the Police must be informed as soon as possible. The person reporting their concerns must ensure that any material evidence is retained and should not influence any police investigation.

ii. Upon receiving a report of suspected use or selling of an illegal substance, the District Commissioner/Centre Proprietor should carry out an immediate investigation of the incident and the circumstances in which it occurred, and then decide upon the appropriate action to be taken. This will include:

- Informing the Member's parents/guardians
- Informing The Pony Club Area Representative who in turn will inform The Pony Club Office
- Informing the Police
- Suspending the Member concerned while investigations are completed
- Awaiting the completion of Police investigations and actions

Disciplinary Action

The normal disciplinary procedure should be followed in cases relating to alcohol or drugs, which can be found in The Pony Club Handbook.

10. DISQUALIFICATION

The Chief Umpire may disqualify a competitor at any stage of the competition:

a. for dangerous riding, or

b. if, in his opinion, the horse is lame, sick or exhausted, or

c. for misuse of whip, spur or bit, or ill-treatment of the horse, or

d. for any breach of the rules, or

e. for unseemly behaviour, including bad language

11. SPONSORSHIP

In the case of competitors and horses, no form of advertising, and this includes a sponsor's name, may appear on the competitor's or horse's clothing and equipment at any Pony Club competition. This does not preclude the wearing of clothing for horses or riders that has been presented by sponsors of the Championships in the current or previous years.

Sponsors at Area Competitions must not be business competitors of the main sponsor of the sport and must be approved by The Pony Club Office. Any advertising material that is used by sponsors, whether it be in the form of display banners or programme material, must be tasteful and not inappropriate to the image of The Pony Club.

12. INSURANCE

The Pony Club 'Public and Products Liability Insurance' Policy includes cover for all the official Area Competitions and the Championships. Details of this insurance are available on The Pony Club website.

In the event of any accident, loss or damage occurring to a third party or to the property of a third party (including the general public and competitors) no liability should be admitted, and full details should be sent at once to The Pony Club Office.

The following statements should be included in all event schedules:

13. HEALTH AND SAFETY

Organisers of this event have taken reasonable precautions to ensure the health and safety of everyone present. For these measures to be effective, everyone must take all reasonable precautions to avoid and prevent accidents occurring and must obey the instructions of the organisers and all the officials and stewards

14. LEGAL LIABILITY

Save for the death or personal injury caused by the negligence of the organisers, or anyone for whom they are in law responsible, neither the organisers of this event or The Pony Club nor any agent, employee or representative of these bodies, nor the landlord or his tenant, accepts any liability for any accident, loss, damage, injury or illness to horses, owners, riders, spectators, land, cars, their contents and accessories, or any other person or property whatsoever. Entries are only accepted on this basis.

15. SPECTATOR AREAS

Horses/ponies are not allowed in any designated spectator only areas at Tournaments. Signs to this effect, e.g. 'No horses' should be erected. It is important to have clearly defined areas where horses/ponies can be worked

PART 2 – RULES FOR THE PONY CLUB POLOCROSSE CHAMPIONSHIPS

16.   ELIGIBILITY

a)   The District Commissioner/Centre Proprietor is required to certify that both horse and rider are eligible to compete under the rules of The Pony Club. Should a breach of eligibility subsequently be discovered, then the Sport Committee may disqualify the offending team or individual.

b)   **Players** – All competitors entered are active members of the stated Branch or Centre to be eligible to compete at the Qualifiers and at the Championships. All competitors are expected to have attended a qualifying tournament to be eligible for the Championships.

c)   **Ponies** – must be sound and in good condition, well shod or with their feet properly dressed. They must not kick or show dangerous vices. They must be at least four years old to play in tournaments. No stallions are allowed.

A horse or pony shall be deemed to reach the age of 1 on the 1st January following the date on which it is foaled and shall be deemed to become a year older on each successive 1st January.

A player is allowed only one pony in a class. A substitute pony can only be used in the event of lameness or accident and with the permission of the Chief Umpire.

d)   **Vaccinations**

A valid passport and vaccination record:

- must accompany the horse/pony to all events
- must be available for inspection by the event officials
- must be produced on request at any other time during the event

All ponies/horses must be compliant with the current Pony Club minimum vaccination requirements - please see the website for the current rule.

Note: Events that are held at other venues may be subject to additional specific rules. For example, any horse/pony entering a Licensed Racecourse Property must comply with the Vaccination requirements as set by the British Horseracing Authority. Similar restrictions apply in the cases of certain polo venues. If you are intending to compete under FEI Rules you will need to ensure you are compliant with those Rules.

17.   MIXED/AREA TEAMS/SECTIONS

When Branches and Centres are unable to raise a team or section from amongst their own Members, or have excess players, the team manager/individual should apply to the organiser who will, where possible, arrange a mixed Branch/Centre team.

Any Area team or section must initially be approved by the relevant Polocrosse Area Co-ordinator. In the event of the Area not having an allocated Polocrosse Area Co-ordinator then the team/section must be approved by The Pony Club Polocrosse Chairman. Final ratification of any Area team/section remains with the tournament organisers.

18.   BRANCH/CENTRE/AREA MANAGERS

An adult Manager should be named with the entry. They are responsible that the members are presented for inspection and ready to play at the appointed time. They must report the team's/section's arrival to the Organiser and confirm names and positions of players.

19.   CHAMPIONSHIP CLASSES

Branches may make entries in any of classes 2, 3 or 4, but no rider or pony may compete in more than one team in the same class. A rider may compete in two classes, providing they are eligible, but not on the same pony.

Class 1 – The Malden Championship

The Malden Championships trophy is presented to the Branch, Centre or Area team that is the most successful overall in the Charles Mason Open Seniors and Stoneleigh Open Juniors classes. This trophy was designed to reward Branches, Centres and Areas who develop sections at both the Senior and Junior level. These sections should work together and support each other to achieve the best overall results. In the event of a Branch, Centre or Area having more than one section in each class they must nominate in advance which sections make up their Malden Championships team.

Teams do not have to enter the Malden Championships, they should enter Class 2 or Class 3 and, providing they have an eligible combination of teams, they will be automatically entered in the Malden Championships.

Class 2 – The Charles Mason Senior Championship

Horses 138cm and over. Open Sections of 3 players of any age.

Class 3 – The Stoneleigh Junior Championship

Players 15 years and under, horses any height. Sections of 3 players who have not attained their 16th birthday by 1st January in the current year.

Class 4 – The Brookes Mini Championship

Players 12 years and under and horses 138cm and under. Sections of 3 players who have not attained their 13th birthday by 1st January in the current year.

In the event of sufficient entries and entered teams consisting of a range of abilities then the classes can be split into Novice, Intermediate and Open levels. Branches, Centres and Areas can request to be entered in a particular level. The Organising Committee has final say as to which sections enter each level, based on each section's respective grading.

The Organising Committee can also insist that a player plays a particular position, for example where a section has two novice level players and one open level player they may insist that the open level player plays a number 2.

In all Classes in the event of a Branch/Centre losing a section member for whatever reason that section must fill the vacant place from other eligible Members from the same Branch/Centre before looking to another Branch/Centre for replacements. The Organising Committee has the final say on team/section composition when sections are mixed.

20.   ENTRIES

a)   Entries for sections/individuals who have qualified for the Championships should be made via the online entry system as per the schedule.

Competing Branches are to supply one Steward per section to be named on the entry. Furthermore, Branches are to supply the services of one Umpire and one horse, trained to stick and ball for the Umpires. Branches unable to supply an Umpire will be allocated one by the Umpire co-ordinator, but must still supply suitable horses and pay the expenses of the allocated Umpire.

NO LATE ENTRIES will be allowed, but eligible substitutions will be allowed at the discretion of the Organiser.

21. WITHDRAWALS (for all Competitions)

If a Branch or Centre withdraws a team or individual prior to the closing date for a competition, a full refund of entry and stabling fees will be made, less an administration charge. Withdrawals after the closing date for a competition will not be refunded.

22. ABANDONMENT (for all Competitions)

In the event of a competition being abandoned, for whatever reason, a refund of 50% of the entry fee will be given. In such an instance the refund process will be communicated and must be followed.

23. MEASUREMENT OF PONIES/HORSES

If an objection to the height of a pony / horse is raised during the course of the Championships, then the Jury of Appeal may request that the animal is subsequently measured according to the rules of the Joint Measurement Board Ltd.

In reaching their decision as to whether to refer the pony/ horse for official measurement, the referees may request the advice of the tournament veterinary surgeon, and it is a condition of entry that the owner, or his representative, will allow that veterinary surgeon to measure the pony/horse on the ground at the time of the tournament. The measurement by the tournament veterinary surgeon will be used for advice only and will remain confidential to the referees and owner and will not be available to the official measurer of the JMB or any other person.

The fee for the official JMB measurement will be the responsibility of the animal's owner. However, The Pony Club may reimburse part or all of the measurement fee should the animal prove to be within the correct height of the competition. Any additional expenses will be the responsibility of the owner.

Any prizes or awards won by the team, which includes the pony subject of the objection, will be forfeit if the animal is proved to be of the incorrect height.

24. OBJECTIONS AND PROTESTS

Apart from the Chief Umpire, Area Representatives and officials of the competition, only District Commissioners/Centre Proprietors or their nominated representatives are entitled to lodge protests or objections which must be made in writing and addressed to the organiser of the competition or secretary of the championships. They must be accompanied by a deposit of £50 which is forfeited unless the Jury of Appeal decides that there were good and reasonable grounds for them. Protests or objections must be made not later than half an hour after the incident concerned or publication of scores. The Official shall give his decision in the first instance. If this is not accepted, the Jury of Appeal shall give their decision after investigation and this decision is final.

25. TACK AND TURNOUT

There will be a Tack and Turnout competition with rosettes for 1st, 2nd and 3rd placed teams in each class, provided an adequate standard is achieved. Members are expected to dress for the parade as per tack check as the winners are judged on their initial turnout.

PART 3 – PLAYING RULES

These Playing Rules are a simplified version of United Kingdom Polocrosse Association's Rule Book. For anything not covered here, and for more detailed explanations, reference should be made to that Rule Book. In the event of any contradiction or confusion between the below summary and the UKPA rule book then the UKPA rule book is considered to be the definitive source for playing rules. Umpires and Instructors should be in possession of a copy.

a) **Stick Side** – the ball may be picked up or caught on either side of the pony, but must be returned to the stick side immediately. It can be carried or thrown. Left-handed players must declare to the umpire before the first throw-in. The umpire will inform the opposing players. The ball can be thrown in any direction and the stick and ball can be taken across the centre line of the pony in the action of throwing or catching, but AT NO OTHER TIME, i.e. the stick must not cross the centre line of the pony to evade a tackle.

b) **Tackles** – a player with the ball in his net may have his stick hit 'upwards' one swing at a time only. When tackling, a player may not cross his opponent's centre line of pony, but may cross his own centre line. To hit a stick 'downwards' is a foul (as it might hit the pony).

Any swing of the stick not upwards is very dangerous and must be penalised immediately. The advantage rule cannot apply here.

Any wild swinging of the stick is a serious foul.

A player must not hit his or any other pony with the stick. Any hit to the horse is penalised by a free goal being awarded against the player who committed the foul.

c) **Intimidation** – any play which, in the opinion of the umpire, is, or may be, intimidating MUST immediately be penalised. This rule will be strictly enforced when there is an obvious variance in size of ponies.

d) Boundary Lines

- A ball on a side line or base line is 'out'.
- A pony's foot touching a side line or base line while the player is in possession of the ball means the ball is 'out'.
- A player must not deliberately throw the ball out over the side line, nor ride out with it in his stick. If he is ridden off and his pony is about to be pushed over the side line he must try to throw the ball back into the field of play.

e) Penalty Line

- Only attacking No. 1 and defending No. 3 may play across the penalty line.
- The ball may not be carried over the line. No. 1 or No. 3 may throw the ball, let it bounce and pick it up again. They must not have the ball in their sticks when crossing the line. The ball may be thrown across the line between two players without having to bounce.
- A player not allowed to play in the goal scoring area may ride over the line, but must not interfere in any way with play and must leave the area immediately.
- A ball at rest on the penalty line is in the centre playing area and must be picked up from that side without the pony's foot going onto or across the line.
- A pony's foot touching the penalty line while the player is in possession of the ball is a foul.

f) Goal Scoring Area

- No. 1 only may score goals from within the goal scoring area, and outside the 10m semi-circle.
- It must be a definite attempt at goal.
- If No. 1 throws at goal and the ball touches No. 3 or his pony, yet goes between the goal posts, it is a goal. Likewise if the No. 3 intercepts and catches the ball being thrown at goal and his pony's foot crosses the line between the goal posts, while the ball is in his net, it is a goal.
- If No. 1 throws at goal and misses, the defending No. 3 restarts the game by throwing the ball in from just behind the penalty line, at a

position in a direct line from where the ball crossed the base line, the ball must travel 10 metres into the midfield.
- If the ball goes out of play over the base line off the No. 1, either as a failed catch or pick-up, there is a throw in from behind the base line by the defending No. 3. Likewise if the No. 3 causes the ball to go out there is a throw-in by the No. 1. If neither player can be held responsible for the ball going out, there is a neutral umpire throw-in between the No. 1 and the No. 3.

g) Line of Ball and Riding Off

- A player following the line of direction of travel of the ball has absolute right of way over a player moving in any different direction.
- A player may not stop or turn on the line of the ball, thereby causing another player to alter course or slow down to evade.
- A player may join the line of ball in front or behind a player already on the line providing it is absolutely safe and he does not obstruct the first player.
- One player may ride another player off the line of the ball but he:

    i. must not come in at an angle that could be dangerous
    ii. must not cause the player being ridden off to be moved laterally at the moment of contact
    iii. must not come in front of opponent's pony's shoulder
    iv. must not come in behind opponent's saddle
    v. must not use his elbows against the opponent
    vi. must not cause a sandwich (i.e. must not come in if there is another pony on the far side)
    vii. must allow a player whom he has ridden off over a boundary line to return immediately to the field of play
    viii. must not be dangerous in any way

- A player must not criss-cross in front of another player's pony, nor ride into another pony's quarters.
- A player wishing to change direction at speed may only cross behind another player so that his pony's nose is well clear of the other pony's tail.
- A player ridden off the field must return within 10 metres of the point he left it and not ride outside the boundary line. He must return to the same area of the field as that which he left.

h) Bad Language

The Umpire shall stop the game and warn the offender; if this continues he shall award a penalty, or, if necessary, send the player off the field.

i) Penalties

Penalties usually take the form of a free throw which must travel at least 10 metres. Other players must be at least 10 metres from the spot where the throw is to be taken. The player taking the free throw may either attempt to pass the ball to a team mate or they can throw the ball and then re-gather it themselves once it has touched the ground. If they opt to do this then they must be given first chance to reclaim the ball and must be given a clear opportunity to do so without interference from opposition players. If they make an attempt to re-gather the ball and fail or the ball travels more than 10 metres then other players may attempt to gather it.

If the player taking the throw plays the ball before it has travelled close to 10 metres, or the ball fails to travel close to 10 metres, or the throw fails in some other way, the umpire shall throw in from the nearest side-line.

In the event of any doubt then the benefit of the doubt should be given to the player taking the penalty throw, in order to allow them the advantage the penalty throw is meant to gain them.

Penalty throws can be given:

i. From the place at which the foul was committed.
ii. From the next penalty line (normally where the team already had possession and was fouled and so to actually give them advantage the penalty throw is moved up the field).
iii. From directly in front of the goal.

For serious or repeated fouls a penalty goal can be awarded or the player sent off the field for a specified time.

The Umpire decides on the severity of the foul and awards the penalty accordingly. If a foul is not dangerous then the advantage rule may be applied, i.e. if the fouled team would be penalised by being given a penalty, the umpire need not stop play. If, during a multi-chukka game, a penalty throw is awarded so near the end of the chukka that there is not enough time to take the penalty throw during that chukka then the throw will be taken at the beginning of the next chukka (and therefore by the other section).

If the game is a single chukka one, or the chukka is the last one of a multi-chukka game, and a penalty throw has been awarded at the end of the chukka in the goal scoring area, then enough extra time will be allowed by the umpires to enable the throw to be taken but no further play to ensue, i.e. a throw directly at goal from the spot indicated by the umpire will be permitted.

ANY PLAYER PLAYING DANGEROUSLY OR PERSISTENTLY FOULING SHOULD BE ORDERED OFF THE FIELD BY THE UMPIRE.

j) Ball Out of Play

The ball is out of play if it touches the boundary line or if, while carrying the ball, a player's horse's hoof touches the boundary line.

i. Over the side line

If the ball is thrown, carried or caused by a player's stick to go over the side line the opposing team will restart play with a penalty throw from the spot where the ball left the field. The ball must travel at least 10 metres in any direction. The throw is to be taken from just outside the field, the player may be moving. All other players to be on the field at least 10 metres from where the throw is to be taken. Other rules pertaining to penalty throws also apply here.

ii. Over the base line

- If the ball is thrown, carried or caused by a player's stick to go over the base line, but is not an attempt at goal by the No. 1, the opposing player will restart play with a penalty throw from the spot where the ball left the field. The ball must travel at least 10 metres into the field. The other rules pertaining to penalty throws apply here.

- Should an attempt at goal fail and go out of play, either directly or deflected off the "Defence" No. 3, the "Defence" No. 3 will be given a clearing throw on the penalty line at a position directly in line from where the ball crossed the back line. The ball must be thrown at least 10 metres in a forward direction.

The "Attack" No. 1 player of the opposing side must follow the "Defence" No. 3 out of the area and should start just behind the No. 3 and to one side, so their horse's nose is level with the No. 3's horse's hip.

iii. Off a horse

Where the ball goes out off a horse accidentally, the umpire will restart play with a line-up from where the ball crossed the line.

k) Outside Assistance

No one may enter the field of play during a chukka to assist a player, e.g. to pick up a dropped stick.

In the event of a bandage coming loose or undone, or if tack breaks during the game, the Umpire will stop play. The pony must leave the field and will not be allowed to return until it has been securely re-bandaged or the broken tack replaced. The Umpire will hold play for a reasonable time for this to be effected, and will then re- start play with a penalty throw for the opposite team.

While cheering on a team is to be encouraged, specific instructions during play are not allowed.

The Umpire may award a penalty against the team concerned for outside assistance.

26. INSTRUCTIONS FOR GOAL JUDGES

- Goals can only be scored by the No. 1.
- Ball to go between the goal posts AT ANY HEIGHT.
- The No. 1 must be inside the goal scoring area and outside the D semi-circle in front of goal when throwing ball.
- It must be a deliberate throw at goal.
- If in doubt tell the Umpire what happened. The ultimate decision is theirs.
- If goal is scored wave the flag or your hand above your head. If goal is missed, wave the flag or your hand below knee level.
- Signal a no goal if No. 1 is inside D when throwing.
- Watch base line and hold flag up, keeping it still, if horse steps on or over baseline while player has ball in his stick.

Only two approved Goal Judges are to be behind the goal posts, preferably wearing high visibility jackets/waistcoats and hard hats. The area is to be kept clear of spectators at all times.

Station yourself between the goal posts and a few yards back. For high balls it is necessary to imagine lines extending upwards from the goal posts, and to decide whether the ball passed between these lines. To do this Goal Judges should be ready to move to be in line with the oncoming ball. It is virtually impossible to judge a fast, high ball correctly otherwise.

27. POLOCROSSE FIELD

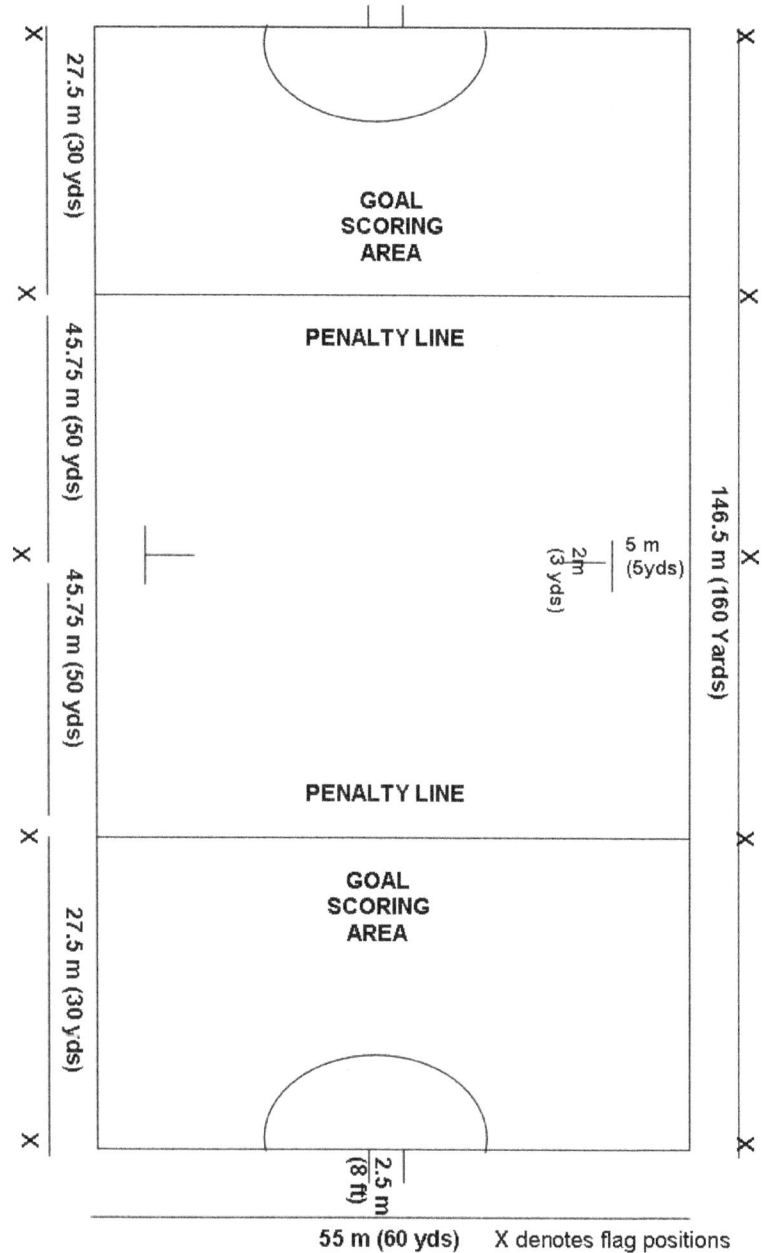

28. EXAMPLE OF FIELD RULES

Example 1

Crossing

A throws the ball to X.

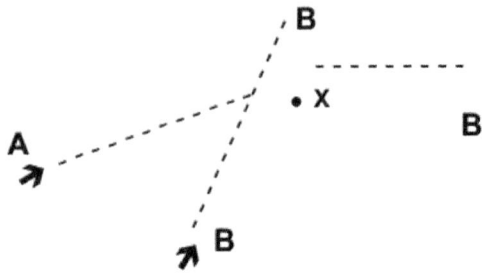

If B can unquestionably reach the ball at X without causing A to check to avoid a collision, then B is entitled to possession and can pick up the ball.

If there is reasonable doubt, then it is B's duty to swerve towards B' (the line of the ball) and attempt a near-side pick up, but if in doing so his horse crosses the line of the ball in the slightest degree then a "cross" is incurred.

Example 2

Crossing

The ball has been thrown to X. Neither A, nor B have thrown it there.

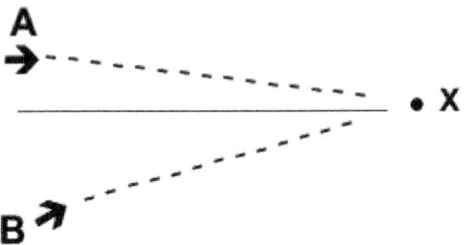

If A and B start riding towards the ball and a collision seems probable, B shall give way to A because A has followed more closely the line on which the ball has travelled.

Example 3

B on the ball throws to X and swings around in a semi-circle. A is following the line of the ball.

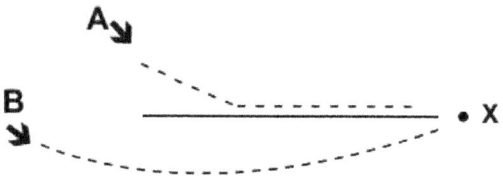

A collision at X is imminent.

Although B threw the ball, he loses possession because A has ridden on a line closer and more nearly parallel to the line on which the ball has been travelling.

A is entitled to possession of the ball and must be given way to.

Example 4

Crossing

No. 1 WHITE in possession of the ball throws to X.

All three players ride for the ball, No. 2 WHITE riding off the No. 3 BLACK all the way and a collision between the three is imminent at X.

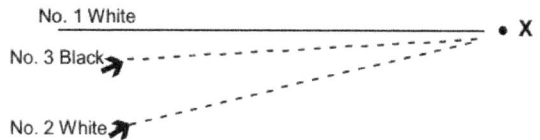

No. 1 WHITE is entitled to possession. A dangerous foul should be given against No. 2 WHITE if he causes No. 3 BLACK to cross No. 1 or if he causes the Defence to pull up so as to avoid a collision with No.1.

APPENDICES

APPENDIX A – HEAD INJURY AND CONCUSSION FLOWCHART

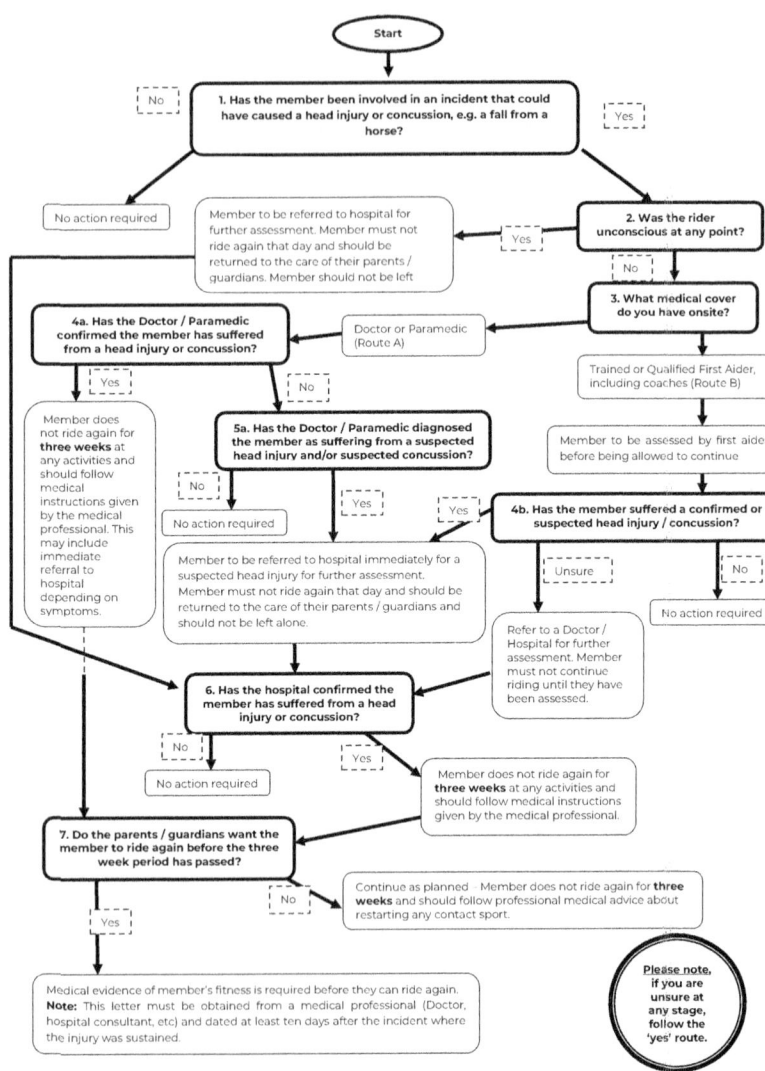

APPENDIX B – SUGGESTED KEY FOR LEAGUE TOURNAMENTS

4 Sections 6 chukkas	4 Sections 6 chukkas	6 Sections 15 chukkas
A v B C v D 10 min gap A v D B v C 10 min gap A v C B v D	A v B C v D E v A B v C D v E A v C B v D E v C D v A E v B	A v B E v C C v D D v F E v F E v A B v C B v D A v F F v C D v E B v E C v A D v A B v F

9 Sections 36 chukkas	8 Sections 28 chukkas	7 Sections 21 chukkas
A v B G v D C v D F v H E v F C v J G v H A c E J v B B v F A v C D v H D v F G v A E v G J v F H v J B v D A v D G v C B v E H v E C v F J v D G v J A v F H v A B v G B v C C v H D v E E v J F v G J v A H v B C v E HH	A v B F v H C v D B v G E v F A v D G v H C v F A v F H v E B v E B v D C v H F v G D v G A v C F v B B v H A v E E v G C v G D v F D v H A v H A v G B v C C v E E v D	A v B G v D C v D A v E E v F B v F G v A G v C C v B A v F D v E D v B F v G G v E A v D C v A B v E G v B C v F E v C D v F

Printed in Great Britain
by Amazon